Where Does
the Water Come From?

Aminjon Shookuhi

Translated by
Karim Khodjibaev and Moukhabbat Khodjibaeva

Illustrated by
Jan Seabaugh

VSP

Dedicated to the memory of Aminjon Shookuhi on his 85th birthday

ISBN 978-0-9740551-2-1

Library of Congress Control Number 2008921226

Viveca Smith Publishing

McKinney, Texas

The Month of Asad

What month is the hottest? Of course, you would say, it's July. In the Tajik language, the word for July is Asad, which is also the word for lion— the most powerful of the animals. That is how powerfully hot July can be in Tajikistan!

In the month of Asad, apples, apricots, and plums ripen. Tomatoes turn red and cucumbers grow sweet in the gardens. Throughout Tajikistan, Asad brings hot weather, and hot weather brings the harvest. That is why the boys and girls in the village of Laklakon sing this song:

When Asad comes
We pick the plums
And fill the baskets
One by one,
And laugh and sing
Until we're done.

It is a nice song—very cheerful. However, one boy does not like it at all. That boy's name is Asad. He thinks that this song is a joke just to tease him. That is why Samad never sings it. Asad and Samad are not only neighbors, but best friends.

They are boys just like any boys—pleasant and friendly. The adults in the village often hold them up as examples to the other children, but Asad and Samad are not goody-goodies. They can be mischievous at times, too.

4

One day in the month of Asad, it had been hot since morning. So what is the best thing to do when it's hot? Swim, of course! For that reason, Samad, as usual, showed up in Asad's front yard.

In Laklakon, as in every other Tajik village, ditches run from one household to the next, bringing water to each. These water channels are built with clay walls. Streams of cool, clean water flow along these ditches. However, when Asad and Samad ran over to the ditch, they found no water in it. So they sat in the damp sand and began to build sand castles and streets. In their sand town, they dug tiny water ditches, too. Every town needs ditches. What would people do without them? Everyone needs water!

Kalta, the puppy, was jumping around and playing with the boys. He soon became bored with this. He wanted Samad and Asad to run with him, but the boys didn't want to run.

They were waiting for the water. After an hour, they heard the splash of the oncoming water. Hurray! "The water has come!" the two friends cheered. They took off their shirts and jumped into the stream. The puppy jumped in, too, because he loved to swim, as well.

Some chickens had been gathering under the pomegranate tree. They seemed to be chattering about something important. They were startled by the noise and looked over at Kalta with scorn.

Chickens are so weird. No matter how hot the weather is, they never swim.

"Why won't they swim?" Samad wondered aloud.

"They are afraid of getting their feathers wet," Asad answered with confidence.

"But it's hot; their feathers would dry back out in no time!" Right away Samad had an idea. "Let's make them swim! They probably just never tried. Once we train them, they will swim by themselves. They will get used to it."

How "innovative" Samad is!

"Okay, let's," Asad agreed, "but we have to start with the rooster. I think the rooster is their chief. Once the chickens see the rooster swimming, they will run to get in the water themselves."

The two friends began chasing the rooster. Catching him turned out not to be easy. The boys exhausted themselves, but still they could not capture the "chief." Even Kalta, who had been helping the boys tirelessly, had his tongue hanging out, panting very hard.

"The rooster is silly. He doesn't understand anything," Samad said. "Let's catch the hen. She may be smarter."

So they caught a speckled hen and put her into the water. She did not like swimming. She flapped her wings and cackled desperately. The other chickens ran back and forth in the yard. It was as though they were asking each other, "A hen in the water?! How could that be? How could that be?"

The rooster began crowing as if he were summoning not only all the chickens of the village, but the people, too. Kalta liked the situation, barking as he watched the fun. Asad and Samad were too busy to hear. It was all they could do keep hold of the hen.

"Don't be afraid," Samad persuaded the hen.

Asad was urging her on, too. "Swim with your paws!"

The hen, however, ignored them and cackled as loudly as she could. By now the yard was very noisy, with the rooster crowing, the chickens cackling, and Kalta barking.

"Oh, Asad is getting into mischief again," thought Gulroo, Asad's mother. Drying her hands on her apron, she stepped out of the house into the front yard.

"What is this?" she shouted. "Why are you bothering the hen? Let her go right this instant!"

"We are teaching her to swim," Asad answered. "She could die without water in this hot weather!"

"But the hen is not a fish," Asad's mother declared firmly.

"Aunt Gulroo, can you tell us why chickens never swim?" Samad asked.

Gulroo smiled and said, "They do swim, but not in the water, but in the sand. They cool themselves off by kicking sand around themselves. Haven't you seen them do this yourself?"

The boys looked at each other and released the hen. She shook herself off and rocketed over to the rooster. The rooster was strutting around as if to tell the hen, "Cock-a-doodle-doo, look how good I am! I called Asad's mother for help!"

Gulroo went back inside. Shortly afterward, the cat, Moshone, appeared in the yard. He lay in the shadow and began to lick his fur.

"Let's teach Moshone to swim," Asad suggested. "As far as I know, he has never swum in either water or sand."

"Let's do it!" Samad exclaimed.

The boys approached the cat, but Kalta did not. He was kind of scared of Moshone. Well, maybe not scared, but he avoided any conflict with that cat.

Moshone did not anticipate any threat, so he did not run away. They lifted him up and took him to the water. Asad was holding his front paws and Samad his back paws.

"One, two, three!" The boys prepared to launch her into the water. But Moshone began to resist. He scratched the boys' hands and escaped.

The two friends began to cry as Moshone bounded off. Kalta was looking at the boys with kindly eyes, as if to say, "Don't you know that Moshone can't get a single joke?"

Hearing all the noise, Gulroo, Asad's mother, went outside again. She listened to the boys and said, "That's good. You won't do any more mischief. You are both big boys, but you act like little babies."

"All good children try to help by watering the flowers and the trees, while you two are busy teaching hens and cats how to swim!"

Then she sent them to wash their hands, and she treated their scratches with iodine. The iodine stung and Asad and Samad were about to cry again. With all that had happened, Samad got fed up and went home.

Asad remained by himself. Well, not all by himself, for his loyal Kalta was with him. It was boring without Samad, though. As Asad walked around in the yard, sore and lonely, he suddenly caught sight of Moshone, sitting on the roof. He threatened Moshone with his fist: "I'll get you!" Kalta, unable to do likewise, just barked angrily.

The next morning there was no water in the culvert again. Asad and Samad went to find some grasshoppers. They caught them and put them in a small match box. When the box was full, they returned to the yard. There Moshone was sitting under the pomegranate tree, washing his face again. The friends approached him. Moshone stood up and looked at them suspiciously, as if asking, "What are you hooligans going to do to me this time?" He was alert and ready to run away any second.

Asad took a grasshopper and tossed it toward Moshone. Then Asad sang,

> Hey, Moshone, hey, Moshone
> Just be our guest
> We brought some food for you
> Just help yourself, Moshone
> Let's make up
> Don't be mad at us any more.

Moshone realized that the boys wanted to make up. He smelled the grasshopper that they offered him, but he did not eat it. Was it, perhaps, that Moshone would not forgive them? No, he forgave them; he simply did not eat grasshoppers. The chickens, however, seeing their favorite food, ran over and quickly ate up all the grasshoppers. So the speckled hen forgave the boys, too. Only the rooster remained distrustful and kept his distance from Asad and Samad.

As noon arrived, it got even hotter. The boys got thirsty and stepped into the house. Gulroo made them lunch. Sometimes after a hot meal on a hot day, you get even hotter. So Samad told Asad, "Whenever the water comes, we have to go swimming."

"Why wait? Let's go and release the water ourselves," Asad suggested.

"From where?"

"From Taheer-bobo's yard. The water always comes from his house."

All of the houses in Laklakon are surrounded by walls made of clay mud. Each house has its own culvert that is connected to another via a small pass under the wall. That pass, which is just a little hole, is called a water pass. The pass under Asad's wall connected the culvert in his yard to the culvert in Taheer-bobo's yard.

Asad took his small shovel and went to the culvert, which had a wooden screen to keep the chickens from using it to escape the yard. The boys returned to the gate, went out into the street, and walked to the neighbor's house. Samad's family lived to the right of Asad's house and Taheer-bobo was Asad's neighbor to the left.

Taheer-bobo, a retired older man, was usually at work in his garden. His cucumbers, tomatoes, and melons were ripe and ready to eat before those of other households. Taheer-bobo hated chickens and considered them his enemies, for they would peck at his young plants.

When the boys appeared in his yard along with Kalta, Taheer-bobo immediately guessed the reason.

"Is it about the water?" he asked.

"Yes," they answered.

"No water today," Taheer-bobo told them. "It didn't come."

"What do you mean?"

"Just what I said. It didn't come and that's it."

The boys persisted. "Where does it come from?"

But Taheer-bobo had no time for lengthy conversations. He said, "The water comes from Burhon the Quince's house. Go there."

Ten minutes later, they were at Burhon the Quince's house. "Burhon the Quince"—what an interesting name! Why do people call him that? Is his yard just a garden of quinces, or does he grow a unique type of quince? The boys got into Burhon the Quince's yard by climbing through the culvert under the wall. First Kalta went quickly, as any dog does. After the dog, Asad climbed through, too.

It should be mentioned that Asad was a tall, skinny boy, while Samad was a chubby, watermelon-shaped child. When Samad tried to get through the culvert, he made it only halfway and then got stuck. Asad tried to pull him out, but that did not work. Realizing that he could be trapped there a long time, Samad began to cry.

The boys were making enough noise that they did not hear the approach of the owner of the house—Burhon the Quince himself. He saw Asad first and shouted, "Now I got you, little troublemaker! Are you here to steal my figs? What family do you belong to?"

"No," Asad responded in his friendliest manner, "we just wanted to find out about the water. Samad got stuck there and- - - - -" He pointed to the culvert. Samad, still stuck, was now numb with fear.

But Burhon the Quince laughed and said, "Oh, poor fellow." Then he helped free Samad from the culvert.

"And now tell me, what are you looking for here?" Burhon asked the two boys in a serious tone.

"We are here for the water!" the boys replied with one voice. Noticing Asad's shovel, Burhon accepted the explanation given by his unexpected visitors. He treated the boys to juicy figs and promised to share his pomegranates with them when they ripened, too. The friends thanked him politely but returned to the reason for their visit.

Asad spoke first. "Uncle," he said, "we found no water in your yard, either. Can you tell us where it comes from before it reaches your house?"

"From the place called Shahtoot," Burhon answered. Shahtoot means Black Mulberry in the Tajik language.

Meanwhile, Samad, who had been enjoying the sweet figs, was examining Burhon's yard curiously. Although there were many plum, pomegranate, and fig trees, there was not a single quince. "That's odd," Samad thought. "Why is this man called Burhon the Quince, then?"

"Where is the quince?" he asked aloud, intrigued.

Adults are never predictable. You never know what you can or can't ask them about. Samad's question upset Burhon the Quince, who suddenly threw a fistful of figs. Astonished, the boys fled from this crazy man.

They would have been better off knowing that Burhon the Quince hated quinces. He could not even hear the word without flying into a rage.

People are so different in this world. Some of them cannot abide certain foods. While one might detest quinces, another might not tolerate apricots or onions or even eggs. Some people overreact when anyone even mentions the word for the food they hate.

An agronomist himself, Burhon Maksudov did not know, himself, why he had such a deep-rooted dislike of the quince. Many years earlier, his house still had two quince trees. When the quinces grew ripe, his friends, just to tease him, would send children into his yard to take a few. These friends would even tell unknowing adults to go into his yard to get a taste of a "really good quince." These visitors would have no idea why their request would set Burhon into such a fury. Finally Burhon simply uprooted the innocent plants; however, the word "quince" remained attached to his name for good.

When the boys ran away, Burhon the Quince did not chase them, and he soon calmed down. After watching the boys disappear in the distance, he returned to his gardening.

The children, now knowing the answer of Burhon the Quince, set forth for Shahtoot, or Black Mulberry, to find out where the water comes from.

Monster or Devil?

They followed the narrow channel that emerged from Burhon the Quince's house. It was great fun to run on the cool and silky fresh grass. The channel turned down into the main water ditch and then uphill again, which brought the boys to an old wall. It was just an old wall, with no house behind it. A big loop was nailed to the bottom of the wall, and a huge bull was tied to the loop by a long rope.

The narrow channel ran along this wall. Following it, the three of them—Asad, Samad, and Kalta—stopped suddenly. They had never seen a giant bull like that before. The bull turned his face angrily toward them and began to paw at the ground with his big hooves. Then he bellowed through his nose in such a terrifying way that they all understood instantly that he was upset about having been disturbed.

Kalta was fast. He made it past the bull, right under his nose. The bull, having missed him, became even angrier than he was. Now sitting on the other side, Kalta seemed to be challenging the boys: "So what are you waiting for? Come on, you can do it, just run."

Asad could consider giving it a shot, but he worried whether Samad could do it, too. Asad was light and quick, but how could he leave Samad?

"We shouldn't tease him," Samad said. "He is so angry."

"Let's fool him," Asad suggested. "We can bring him some food, and while he eats, we can run past him."

"Sure," agreed Samad.

They brought some tree leaves, and the bull changed his mood. They got by safely as he ate.

Shahtoot is a unique place. Lots of bushy mulberry trees grow here with juicy sweet mulberries on them. With the bull now calmly eating, the boys continued into Shahtoot. They found a little mound among the trees. The horns of a wild sheep were resting on that mound. "It could be an old grave that someone left these horns to mark," the boys thought. Traditionally something is left on top of a grave.

Three water streams crossed over Shahtoot, the main one and then two smaller ones. There was no water in any of them. Not in a single one. A bit farther, a man was sleeping under the shadow of the largest mulberry tree. He had his robe wadded up to make a pillow.

The man was sleeping soundly and did not take any notice of anything around him. He did not even feel how the mulberries dropped on his face. As they fell on him, they smashed on his face, staining him a purple-red color. He was snoring loudly. To the boys, he sounded like a bullfrog. They backed away from him and began to pick some fruit. Kalta was ignoring this process. Who knows?—maybe he was as touchy about mulberries as Burhon was about quinces.

"Maybe this uncle is a guard," Samad suggested. "Maybe he is supposed to guard Shahtoot, but he is sleeping."

"Why would anybody steal mulberries?" Asad disagreed.

"The black mulberry is a treatment for tonsillitis," Samad said.

"No, the treatment for tonsillitis is....well, I forget what, but it isn't the black mulberry," Asad countered.

"Yes, it is," Samad argued.

They got into an argument.

Then they heard a voice behind them. "So are the black mulberries sweet enough?"

Asad and Samad whirled around. There stood another man, looking at the one who was asleep under the tree.

"Hey, boys, do you want me to show you a monster?" the man asked them.

Of course, the two friends wanted that. "Show us, show us!" they urged.

The new man carefully took the horns from the mound and placed them above the head of the sleeping man. They made him look scary.

"Well, what does he look like?" the new man asked them.

"He looks like a dragon," Samad said.

"No, it's the devil," Asad said, "The devil comes with horns."

"To me he looks like a monster," the man said. "Don't wake him up. Let him sleep. I'm leaving."

The boys took a seat on the ground and impatiently waited for Tavakkalhoja to wake up. Meanwhile, an older woman and younger one appeared in fine dress, apparently on their way to a party. The younger one had a round plate on her shoulder, where she carried sweets and pastries.

Talking to one another as they passed, they might not have noticed the sleeping man, and that's why Asad pointed and whispered, "Hey, look, there is a sleeping monster!"

"Mommy!" the young woman cried and streaked back to her mother. The plate full of sweets and pastries fell loudly from her shoulder to the ground. Her mother began to pray earnestly. The sleeping man—Tavakkalhoja— woke up, and when he discovered the horns on top of his head, he jumped up like a rabbit.

Now the woman and her daughter recognized the "monster" and calmed back down.

"For God's sake," the old woman said to him. "Who did this to your face? Look at yourself." She opened her bag and gave him a little mirror. Tavakkalhoja became very angry.

"Who did this to me?" He was ready to punish anyone.

"Oh, poor baby," the old woman said. "It's true what they say: Sleep is the brother of death. I guess these two mischief-makers did this, making you look like a dead man instead of a sleeping one. That was wrong of them."

Asad and Samad wound up getting blamed for everything that had happened. Tavakkalhoja moved toward them. The boys took off running.

Kalta was fast, too. All three raced by the bull that was still at the channel along the wall. When Tavakkalhoja came by, though, in pursuit of the boys, the bull pulled on the rope so hard that he tore it out.

Now Tavakkalhoja was in trouble. The bull was really after him. Tavakkalhoja, whose face was still mulberry-red as a monster's, had a hard time running. The bull could reach him at any moment, and it was dangerous. Any second the bull could sweep him up by the horns.

"Help!" Tavakkalhoja yelled as loudly as he could. Hearing his cries, some adults who had been working nearby rushed to help. They managed to stop the bull. After securing the bull, they found Tavakkalhoja's face very funny and laughed.

Finally, when the people dispersed, Asad and Samad returned to Shahtoot and inspected the ditches. They still found no water in any of the three ditches that crossed the Shahtoot.

"Let's follow the biggest one," Samad suggested. "We'll be sure to find water, and we may know then where the water comes from." So they went farther along the water channel. They enjoyed some blackberries, but Kalta did not enjoy the smell of them, and turned his face away.

Peaches

Asad and Samad walked for a very long time. After crossing a cotton field, the ditch brought them to the district orchard. The smell of sweet apples, pears, and peaches was so delicious.

The boys found a big peach tree. They were struck by the beauty of the tree and by the amount of fruit on it. However, the peaches were not yet ripe. But who can restrain themselves when the peaches are right in front of them? Both Asad and Samad wanted to taste at least one peach.

"Wow! Look at those peaches," Asad said.

"Let's try them," Samad suggested boldly.

"What if the security guard sees us?"

Samad answered at once. "Let's bend one branch down, collect the peaches, and then eat them somewhere else." Both boys tucked their shirts into their pants and began to stuff peaches down inside their shirts.

They were busy picking peaches when they heard a voice: "Hey, be careful! Don't break the branch!"

That was the security guard, an old man who stood by, watching the boys. He was a kind man, and he did not want to scare them. He had been a small boy once himself, and liked peaches, too.

Asad and Samad ran out of the orchard as fast as they could.

"Wait! Where are you going?" the guard called out. "I can help you get better peaches!" But the boys never heard what the guard was saying.

They ran to a safer place, sat down, and began to eat the peaches that they had picked. They offered one to Kalta, but the dog excused himself once more. After they had eaten enough, they still had some peaches left inside their shirts. Soon each of them began to feel itchy all over. At first they said nothing about it to one another, but the itching continued and Samad finally said, "I am itching all over."

"I am, too," Asad responded in a scared voice.

"You know," Samad said, becoming pale, "you and I have contracted the itching disease."

"We will be taken to the hospital and they will give us shots!" Asad said, panicking.

The boys plucked the rest of the peaches out of their shirts, threw them aside, and rushed home. They even forgot about the water that they had been looking for.

"Mommy! Mommy!" Asad cried as he entered the house. "My whole body is itching!"

"Where have you been? What did you eat?" Asad's mother looked worriedly at the rash on his face and hands.

Asad hid some of the truth. He replied, "Nothing really happened. We went to find where the water comes from to our yard, and I was with Samad."

Samad did not disclose the secret, either. His mother, worried, went over to Asad and Gulroo's house. Meanwhile, the two friends kept itching and crying. Finally Gulroo said very categorically, "Asad, dear! If you don't tell us the truth, you will be itching all your life, and no one will help you, not even a doctor! Tell us now, truly, where have you been and what did you eat?"

Having no choice, Asad confessed. Both mothers took a deep breath and relaxed. Now they knew what to do with these "bad boys."

"See? You punished yourselves for stealing those peaches," Gulroo said.

"Who taught you that it was okay to let peaches touch your skin?" Samad's mother said, realizing the problem. Both boys were immediately sent to take a shower. The itching promptly disappeared. In the evening, the boys met back up again.

"You know, Samad," Asad said, "that itching was because of the peaches."

"What we had to do was wash them first. They were fresh from the tree," Samad replied.

"They were clean—that wasn't the problem—but peaches have hairy skin that causes itching. That's what my mom said," Asad continued.

"Now I know that, too," Samad agreed.

"Okay, enough about the peaches," Asad decided. "What do you think? Are we going to look for the water or not?"

"Of course we are. Just don't tell anyone; otherwise, after that business with the peaches, they could keep us at home," Samad said.

"Promise!" Asad said.

At Dushokh

Early the next day, Asad and Samad set forth again on the expedition to find where the water comes from. They had been told to go to the Dushokh area, from which, the people said, the water flows to reach their own village of Laklakon. When they reached Dushokh, however, they didn't find any water. The ditches there were empty, too. Nearby, though, they spotted three men talking to one another.

They recognized Burhon the Quince, Tavakkalhoja, and the man who had played the joke on Tavakkalhoja when he was sleeping. All three men were arguing.

"You, Hasan the Fun, you will see what I can do. Yesterday you made me a "monster" man. You'll pay a high price for your silly jokes. I'll pay you back with a practical joke of my own sometime soon."

So the boys learned that the trickster's name was Hasan the Fun.

"Hey, Tavakkalhoja," Burhon the Quince said, "stop making those empty threats. Year after year I hear the same things from you."

"I'm not talking to you, you sour quince," Tavakkalhoja answered.

"What did you just say?" Burhon asked him angrily.

Just then a man on a horse approached the three men. It was the mirab—the official whose job it is to regulate the water flow to the community ditches. The boys recognized him instantly, even though they had never seen him before. They had always heard from adults that the mirab had a long brushy mustache and that his name was Muhammadjon.

They also knew that the mirab has a very important job—to decide which field gets water first and for how long. The boys looked at this man with great admiration.

"What's wrong?" the mirab asked the three men who were standing there.

"It's my turn to receive the water," Tavakkalhoja said, "but Hasan is arguing with me about it."

"No, it's my turn," Hasan said, "and Tavakkalhoja had better have another nap. He won't sleep long—just a couple days."

"He used to sleep all the time," the mirab remarked, and everyone laughed. Tavakkalhoja felt embarrassed and lowered his head.

Meanwhile, Asad and Samad grew more and more bewildered. What water were these adults talking about? What water did they want to bring into their fields? There wasn't a single drop of water around.

They could not muster the courage to ask the mirab, so they went to Tavakkalhoja and asked him, "Uncle, where does the water come from?"

"From your nose!" Tavakkalhoja responded peevishly.

The boys both sniffed through their nostrils suddenly and took a step backward. The mirab continued seriously, "It's true, the water must go to Tavakkalhoja first. I saw the land in his section. It needs watering. What would you say, Burhon? Am I right?"

"Yes, you are," Burhon, the agronomist, answered.

Burhon had known that Tavakkalhoja needed water immediately, but Hasan the Fun was clever and liked to argue, even with the odds against him. But now the mirab himself settled the question. Hasan the Fun looked disappointed, but Tavakkalhoja was happy to hear the mirab's decision. He looked over at Hasan as if to say, "So there."

Why do adults sometimes act like children, anyway? Is it, perhaps, because they were children once, themselves?

Eventually the mirab left. Hasan the Fun and Burhon the Quince left, too.

Then Tavakkalhoja took his shovel. He began to cut open a channel to release the water into his ditch. The boys sat down nearby to observe his work. They wanted to witness how the water flowed into another stream.

Suddenly Tavakkalhoja put his shovel down, walked up to the boys, and pulled off their hats, saying, "Aren't you the ones who made fun of me yesterday and then ran away? You little rascals! I should keep your hats, and sell them at the market."

"We didn't do it!" the boys cried out. "That was Uncle Hasan the Fun," they said.

"I know. I know that Hasan did it, but why didn't you wake me up?" He waited a moment, then said, "It's okay. You can make it up, of course. Just go and do this job for me." And so Asad and Samad began to dam the water for Tavakkalhoja's stream.

38

While they worked hard, Tavakkalhoja went in the shadow of a mulberry tree and fell asleep. Very soon the boys heard a loud snore. They tiptoed up to him, but he was sleeping soundly.

"Let's take our hats back," Samad whispered.

"What if he wakes up?" Asad asked doubtfully. "Then he'll never give us our hats back."

"No, he is sleeping soundly," Samad said again.

So they pulled their hats out of his hands. Then they became even more courageous.

"Let's tie his feet together with his belt," Samad said. Samad was quite "creative."

"Great idea," Asad agreed. They tied Tavakkalhoja's feet together with his belt and fled. Kalta was happy to run again. Pleased with what they had done, the boys continued up the big water channel, with no knowledge of where it would go.

Asad Hangs from the Tree

Soon afterward, the boys neared a huge walnut tree. Lots of bird nests were in its heavy branches. As soon as the boys approached, the birds began fussing at them. Samad remembered a riddle he had heard, and told it to Asad:

What flies like an arrow
Sits like a king
Is whiter than milk
And blacker than coal?

"I know what it is!" Asad answered. "It's a magpie! You know, they may still have baby birds in their nests. Let's go up and see them."

"Why?" Samad hesitated. "Would it really be all that interesting? Haven't we already seen baby birds?" Samad did not like to climb trees, and to be honest, he just couldn't do it. Maybe it was because he was such a round and chubby boy.

"Don't be afraid," Asad said, "you stay here, and I'll go by myself. There is no tree that I cannot climb."

"Why should we go up there?" Samad persisted, still against the idea. "Look, the nests are at the very top, where the branches are really small."

Asad was stubborn, though, and up he went. The higher he got, the louder the magpies screeched.

Asad had almost reached the nests. When he looked down, his heart began pounding. Suddenly the branch that he was standing on cracked and broke. Asad hung on by his hands.

"Be careful!" Samad called, stunned.

"Help!" Asad screamed.

"Help!" Samad joined in.

Asad could fall at any moment. Samad looked around and noticed some bundles of hay nearby. Samad quickly began to pile the bundles under the tree. He was so busy hurrying with this task that he did not notice an old man who had been working there also.

"Hey, there! Don't steal my hay!" he shouted over to Samad.

"But, Grandpa, look! Asad will die!"

"What?" the old man said. "Are you teasing me? Asad will live a hundred years!" Samad simply was not aware that this old man's name was also Asad.

Samad just pointed his finger up at Asad in the tree. "There!"

The old man then realized what was going on and joined Samad in piling together bundles of hay. Soon the pile was high enough for Asad to let go and jump down.

"Come on, just do it!" the old man coaxed.

"Come on! Come on!" Samad called to his friend.

Asad finally released his hands and dropped straight down onto the piles of hay. While falling, his shirt blew up like a parachute.

The old man helped him to his feet. "Are you okay? Are you all right?"

Asad was silent. His eyes were blinking and his hair was full of hay stalks.

"He is all right! He is okay!" Samad responded happily.

"Thank God!" the old man said with relief. He sat down on the ground and dried his sweaty face.

"Wow! You were really airborne!" Samad said to Asad. Samad was amazed at what his friend had done.

"I put my hands up on purpose," Asad said, praising himself for his graceful fall. He had recovered his voice by now.

"You had better thank your friend here and not be so self-serving," the old man cautioned Asad. "If he hadn't been here, your hands and feet would have been broken."

"Hey, thanks," Asad said, looking embarrassed. He shook Samad's hand.

Suddenly the old man, who had been so relieved by Asad's safe landing, jumped up as if he had been bitten by a snake. He was upset by what could have happened. "You two mischief-makers!" he cried. "If I ever see you getting up in this walnut tree again, I will pull you down myself."

The boys ran away again, and Kalta, after barking back at the old man a few times, followed them. In a few minutes they found themselves quite far from that place. They looked back. The old man was picking the hay bundles back up and returning them to their places. The friends watched in silence. Each of them realized how lucky they had been to have the old man so near that tree.

Asad spoke first. "Don't tell anyone about what happened, please," he said to Samad. "If my family finds out what happened, they won't let me out for a while."

"I won't tell. Be careful, yourself, not to let it slip," Samad said.

Soon they reached the ditch, when they heard the sound of water. The water had just arrived, and one part of the stream made a little pool, where they decided to swim. They took off their clothes and jumped into the water. They momentarily forgot everything that had happened to them that day. Now they were having fun. Samad was happy to sing:

We run and we run
And get hotter and hotter
To cool off in the water
And have lots of fun.
Only those who are lazy
Don't splash here like crazy!

When Samad sang the word "lazy," both boys suddenly remembered Tavakkalhoja.

"Samad, what do you think?" Asad asked. "Is he still sleeping or has he woken up? The water probably reached him a while ago."

When the boys returned to the Dushokh area, they found another debate in progress.

"I swear to bread!" Tavakkalhoja was shouting. "It was Hasan the Fun who tied my feet together. Hasan and his friends!"

"That is not true," Hasan retorted. "We know nothing. We came here because the water came to our farmland. We did not dam up our water stream or anything. I mean, why didn't Tavakkalhoja turn the water to his section? It must mean that he didn't want to, and tied his own feet together as an excuse."

Tavakkalhoja definitely knew who had tied him up, but to admit to such an embarrassing fact was too much for him. In a moment he noticed the two

culprits, Asad and Samad, standing nearby, listening. His face grew red. He thought to himself, "I'll show them. I'll teach them a lesson."

"Stop making up stories," Burhon the Quince said to Tavakkalhoja.

"I swear to bread it's true," Tavakkalhoja repeated.

"Hey, sleepy, don't swear by bread," people were admonishing Tavakkalhoja. "It's sacred, you know."

"Do you want me to tell you the truth?" Samad asked, approaching the adults. He wanted to help Tavakkalhoja, but he wasn't aware that Tavakkalhoja was hiding the truth on purpose.

"What are you doing here?" Tavakkalhoja said angrily. He made a step toward Samad, but he slid on a slippery rock and fell into the water ditch. The boys had no choice but to flee again.

The Tale About the Water

That evening Asad's grandma, Anorbibi, visited them. Asad was very delighted to see her because he loved her very much.

"My grandma knows lots of stories," he said proudly to Samad. "Make sure to come to my place for a sleepover tonight. We will listen to her tell tales."

After dinner, as dusk was gathering, the boys sat near Asad's grandma, ready to listen. Anorbibi was not sure which story would be best to tell. After the boys had waited patiently for a time, Asad said, "Grandma, tell us the tale about the water."

"Which one? The one about Farhad and Shirin?"

"No," Asad said, "the one about Ohdeel."

"Oh, that one," Anorbibi said. "Good, now listen...."

"Once upon a time, back in the olden days, there was a prosperous town which people had established in the middle of a vast desert. Everyone had a happy life there.

However, one day the Seven-Headed Monster, the master of the desert, was passing by. He was checking out his territory. He discovered the town and became upset. The aroma of flourishing apples and peaches worried his heart. The smell of flowers gave him a headache and made his eyes dim. The laughter of merry people weakened him.

The monster went back to his cave and called his buddies, the Hot Dry Wind and the Tornado. The monster ordered them to ruin that town. Within a few days of straight and whirling winds, the trees and flowers wilted.

A year later, the Seven-Headed Monster was again checking out his territory. He was shocked to see the same town flourishing and prosperous again. The monster became very angry, and this time he drafted all of the worst worms and bugs to invade that place. They attacked the plants and trees and killed them.

Well, what do you think would happen if a year later, the monster discovered the town in good shape again? He became so angry that he decided to ruin that place himself. He lifted a huge mountain and threw it on the town.

A year after that, though, the Seven-Headed Monster found the town living beautifully, and the mountain had been pushed away.

The monster got really puzzled. It was hard to believe that people were stronger than he was, when he was the Seven-Headed Monster and the master of the desert. What could he do? The monster decided to ask for some advice. He went to his teacher, who hadn't left his cave for a thousand years."

"How big was the monster's teacher?" Asad wondered.

"As big as a camel," guessed Samad.

"He was smaller than a mosquito," Anorbibi continued.

Right at this moment, a mosquito appeared, going straight for Asad's nose. He slapped his palms together and said, "Look, I killed the monster's teacher."

"Are you going to listen?" Anorbibi asked, looking at each of the boys. She went on...

"The monster's teacher never left his cave because the sun or the moonlight could kill him. The Seven-Headed Monster entered the cave and greeted his teacher: 'Lattah, pattah, chattah, my Master!'

That meant 'May the darkness be on your side, my teacher.'

The teacher listened to the monster's story and laughed. 'Your efforts were all in vain,' he said. 'You could never ruin the town and kill its residents unless you took their soul. The soul of that place is water. Just get the water, and the town will die.'

The monster accomplished that mission quickly. He went to the area and blocked the main water stream and settled himself to guard it. Very soon the town was in great trouble. The trees and plants yellowed, and the people suffered from thirst. Whenever people tried to bring the water back, they were killed by the Seven-Headed Monster. Nobody was able to defeat the master of the desert.

It must be mentioned that seven brothers lived in that town, and all of them were warriors. Their names were Sunday, Monday, Tuesday, Wednesday, Thursday, Friday, and Saturday. Each of them went to fight the monster and fought for seven days, but each was killed. Soon not a single drop of water remained in the town, and every living thing was dying: the people, the birds, and the animals.

One day a young shepherd whose name was Ohdeel came to his mother and said, "It's my turn now to go and fight the monster. I will kill him and bring the water back to the people."

"Please don't do it!" his mother begged him. "Don't fight the monster; you'll get killed!"

"I have to go," Ohdeel said. "It's better to be killed than to die from thirst."

So he took his knife and went to the spot where the monster was. On his way there, he met a swallow. The swallow asked him where he was going. The boy said that he was going to kill the monster and release the water.

"You are a kind man," the swallow said. "Last year you rescued me from a snake, and now it's my turn to help you. Just know that it is not easy to kill the monster unless you know where his soul is."

"Do you know where his soul is?" Ohdeel asked the swallow.

"I don't, but I'll ask the other birds, and they may know."

The swallow flew to a turtledove. "Do you know where the monster's soul is?"

"I heard that his soul is in his nose," the turtledove replied, "but in which of the seven heads, I don't know."

The swallow flew to a partridge and asked, "Do you know where the monster's soul is?"

"His soul is within his biggest head. There is a worm there, and this worm contains his soul. The pheasant knows how to kill that worm."

The pheasant said, "I know Ohdeel. He never once threw rocks at my nest. Tell him to go to the ants. If they poison the worm, you can pull it out from the monster's nose."

Ohdeel went to the ants and asked them for help. The ants answered, "We will help you because we owe you. Any time you had lunch, you left the crumbs near our house. Just find out when the monster sleeps. Ask the turtle—she knows more."

60

"I will help you," said the turtle when Ohdeel appeared at her residence. "I remember how you protected me from a hawk. You must respond to kindness with kindness. Listen and remember," she said. "The monster falls asleep right at noon. His eyes remain open, but he is actually sleeping."

Ohdeel thanked the turtle and returned to the ants. At night the ant forces advanced. By morning they had reached the mountain where the Seven-Headed Monster was lying, and they hid under the stones.

When noon arrived, the ants entered the sleeping monster's nose and poisoned the worm. After the worm grew dizzy, they pulled it out. They left it right at Ohdeel's feet. Ohdeel took a big stone and squashed the worm. The ground started to shake, lightning struck, and thunder sounded. The Seven-Headed Monster jumped up, screamed, and burnt to ashes.

Everyone soon found out that Odheel had defeated the master of the desert. The people, the animals, the birds, and even the flowers were joyous. The residents restored the flow of water, and it returned to the farms and fields.

Anyone who does good deeds preserves his name for many years. That town was renamed after Ohdeel. It is now called Ohdeelabad, or Justice Town.

And water is the soul of life."

Asad's grandmother finished her story with these words. "Tajiki people say, 'The best deed in the world is to give water to someone who is thirsty.'"

Kalta and Tavakkalhoja Are Heroes

The next morning, Asad and Samad continued their expedition, in search of where the water comes from. They walked fast, and Kalta again was running alongside. They passed all the places they had explored before—Laklakon, Shahtoot, and Dushokh. As they were walking along the road, one of the trucks passing by pulled over to the shoulder. The driver, a family friend from their village, emerged, opened the hood, and looked at the engine. Both boys approached the truck and tried to look at the engine, too. It's always interesting to find out what is wrong with an engine, isn't it?

The driver finished making some adjustment, then asked the boys, "Here is a bucket. Would you mind bringing some water for me?"

Samad grabbed the bucket and ran to the stream. When he returned, the driver asked the boys, "Where are you going?"

"We want to find out where the water comes from," Asad said.

"That means that you need to get to the village of Beadzorr, where the canal is," the driver said. "Get into my truck and I will give you a ride." Both boys and Kalta enjoyed this moment.

"So what do you think," the driver asked later, "which is better—a spacecraft or a truck, huh?"

The boys didn't know what to say. What if they said a spacecraft—would it offend the driver? Asad whispered, "A truck, maybe."

"Tell me the truth: which would you prefer to become, a truck driver or an astronaut?"

"An astronaut!" both boys replied simultaneously.

"Aha, here we go," the driver said. "If you are astronauts, one day will you give me a ride, then?"

"Certainly!"

"For free?"

"Of course, for free."

"Okay, then, I'll give you this ride for free, too," the driver said. He was a very funny and smiley man. In fifteen minutes, he stopped the truck and said, "Here is your destination. The canal is right there, but don't swim there, all right?"

"All right! Thank you, Uncle."

The truck soon left. The canal was quite big, just like the river that Asad and Samad had seen in a movie. The banks of the canal were made of concrete.

There was a sign on one side of the canal. Both boys tried to read what the sign said. It wasn't easy because they had not started going to school yet. Samad, who knew the alphabet, tried to read: "The first letter is D and the second is O."

"The third letter is N," Asad added.

As they were struggling to read the rest of the letters, a girl their age was passing by and loudly said, "Don't Swim in the Canal."

Asad and Samad felt embarrassed, and they lowered their heads as the girl proceeded on her way.

"If you can't swim in the canal, like the sign says, why do I hear kids laughing?"

Asad and Samad came closer and found a group of boys swimming in the canal. Even a very little boy was active, moving back and forth from one bank to the other.

While both boys watched the child swim, some other boys took some clay and covered the first four letters of the sign. Now it read, "Swim in the Canal."

Asad and Samad were jealous of the boys, but they did not join them because of the promise that they had made to the truck driver.

The other children challenged them: "What are you waiting for?" "Come on and join us!" "Take off your shirts!" "Are you afraid of the water?"

"There's no swimming in the canal," Samad said.

"We have an important mission to accomplish," Asad added.

Asad was about to explain to the Beadzorr village boys why they were there, but just then one of the swimmers ran up to him and grabbed his hat. He didn't just take the hat, but he threw it into the canal. Asad and Samad were astonished. Kalta, however, was quick to help. He jumped into the water and brought back the hat.

After another young swimmer took Samad's hat, too, and threw it into the water, Kalta repeated his performance, fetching it, too, from the canal.

All of the other boys hid their hats, just in case. At that moment, the girl who had read the sign for Asad and Samad came walking back. She was wearing a bright and colorful hat on her head, too.

One little mischief-maker was just waiting for this chance. He approached the girl quickly, took off her hat, and threw it into the canal. He then turned to Kalta and said, "Go fetch! Go fetch!"

But Kalta didn't move. He didn't even respond to the boys' commands. By ignoring all their appeals, Kalta seemed to be saying, "Be thankful that I saved your hats, but I am not about to save some girl's hat, even if she can read."

The girl was crying and walking back and forth along the slippery canal bank. Then when she tried to retrieve her hat, bending over, she slipped and fell into the water. It was immediately obvious that she could not swim.

All of the boys froze, unable to move. A man appeared from nowhere and jumped into the canal to rescue her. He helped the girl to get out of the water.

"Go home and don't worry," he said to the girl. "Everything is all right now." He was waist-deep in the water, and when he turned toward the boys, he warned them sternly, "I'll get you kids!" The children disappeared. Meanwhile, Asad and Samad recognized who the man was. Yes, it was Tavakkalhoja!

When Tavakkalhoja tried to get himself out of the canal, it simply didn't happen. The canal banks were slippery, and he couldn't get a good grip on anything to climb out.

He tried a few more times, but did not succeed. Meanwhile, the amount of water in the canal increased. Soon Tavakkalhoja was in water all the

way up to his neck. It was obvious, too, that he could not swim. It was amazing that a man who could not swim could have saved a girl from drowning, but it was so. Asad and Samad neared the water. They felt sorry for Tavakkalhoja. They had not realized that he was so kind and so ready to help a person in trouble. Tavakkalhoja recognized them immediately, too.

"Look, boys," he said in a very friendly tone, "help me out of the water. Just give me your hands."

Asad rushed forward first and extended his hand. Samad followed suit. It didn't help, though, because both boys were so small, and Tavakkalhoja was so big. Tavakkalhoja even took off his shirt for them to grab, but it did not help.

Tavakkalhoja addressed the boys again. "My friends," he said, "go and find a big stick. Don't leave me here alone. Whenever I get out, I'll offer you the sweetest watermelon..."

Tavakkalhoja was reluctant to acknowledge that he could not swim and that he was so uncoordinated. He was afraid of anyone seeing him there, especially Hasan the Fun. Asad and Samad ran to some nearby bushes, where they looked for a long stick to help them pull Tavakkalhoja out of the water. They found a long branch of a tree, and they extended one end of it to Tavakkalhoja. All of the efforts of the two small boys, however, were not enough to pull a big man out of the water.

Finally Samad suggested, "Uncle, what would you think if we asked someone for help?"

"No, no!" Tavakkalhoja said, worried. "Let's take a break and try again."

After a few minutes of rest, they returned to their mission. Asad and Samad pulled on one end of the branch, while Tavakkalhoja held onto the other. Even Kalta joined in to help the boys, pulling on Samad's pants with his teeth. At one point, Tavakkalhoja was almost out of the water, but he lost his balance again, and if the boys had not let go of the branch, they would have wound up in the canal, too.

While they were working, Asad's hat fell into the water, but none of them noticed.

After some time, the mirab Muhammadjon appeared on his horse. He recognized Tavakkalhoja and addressed him sternly. "What is the matter with you, Tavakkalhoja? Instead of preventing children from swimming here, you are showing them a bad example. See, even a blind man can read this sign, can't he?" He pointed to the sign but saw at once that the sign had been changed to mean its opposite.

"Is that your work?" the mirab asked. "Did you change the sign?"

Tavakkalhoja finally had to face what he had been trying to avoid—his inability to swim. The truth was so embarrassing. "No, I was rescuing a girl when she fell into the canal and..."

"That's enough right there," the mirab interrupted. "You can't be telling the truth! What girl? I am sure you fell into the water while sleeping. You can't swim and yet here you are, talking about rescuing someone. I'll tell you that if you can't cook noodles then you don't teach others how to cook them."

"Tavakkalhoja is telling the truth!" the boys said in chorus. "If he had not been here, the girl would have drowned."

The mirab was surprised: Tavakkalhoja, that sleepy, lazy man, saved a girl's life? "All right," he said finally, "maybe you rescued the girl, but then why are you still in the water yourself?"

"I can't get out," Tavakkalhoja confessed. "It's too slippery."

"Well," the mirab suggested, "I can call Hasan the Fun, and he will help you."

"Please don't," Tavakkalhoja said. "He'll make fun of me in front of the entire village."

"Fine, fine," the mirab said. "I will not tell anyone, but then you owe me some pilaf."

"Of course, of course!" Tavakkalhoja replied. "I'll invite you over for the nicest pilaf many times, my friend."

"Oh, my poor fellow," the mirab said as he stepped down from his horse. "Here is my hand." In a moment Tavakkalhoja was back on firm ground.

"Many thanks, Muhammadjon," Tavakkalhoja said to the mirab.

The mirab smiled and set forth again on his horse down the road. Now Tavakkalhoja turned to face the boys.

"You mischief-makers!" he said to them. "Anytime I meet you, it's more trouble for me.

Don't tell me that you didn't push that girl into the water."

"We swear we never did that!" Asad and Samad said in concert. "That girl fell into the water herself. The Beadzorr boys threw our hats in, too."

"Fine, then," said Tavakkalhoja, growing more sympathetic. "Just don't share with anyone what happened today, and I will give you both quails to eat."

"Really?" The boys were happy.

"I promise," Tavakkalhoja said.

"When are we going to get the quails?" Asad asked.

"Maybe tonight I'll set up some traps. Then, if I catch any, those are yours." Actually, Tavakkalhoja wasn't convinced, himself, that he would give the boys quails. He had never hunted quails or any other animal, for that matter. But Asad and Samad believed him, because they wanted the quails.

Alarm

Rumors do not have feet to run, and they don't have wings to fly, but they spread so fast that e-mails and telephones have every reason to be envious. Passing from mouth to mouth, the rumors also get enriched with many added details.

Some people like news and like to circulate rumors. Since they have so little idea of what they are talking about, however, they fill in elements from their own imaginations, and thus spread panic and fears...

This time the subject of the rumors was Asad and Samad. The boys themselves had no clue about this.

Here is what happened:

The boys from Beadzorr who had run away from the canal regrouped nearby. Although they had been scared, they were also curious about what would happen next. Very soon, an old woman approached them, interested in why they were gathered there together.

"A girl fell into the canal," one of the boys told her.

"Oh, my goodness!" the old woman responded. She walked further on her way, still thinking about this bit of news. "That is too bad!" she said. A man who was riding his bike in parallel with this woman asked her what she was talking about.

"A girl just fell in the canal," she replied.

The man on the bike stopped at a store soon afterward, where he shared the news with his buddy, the shop owner. "Have you heard this? I think a boy fell in the canal or something…"

A few minutes later, in the neighboring teahouse, the shop owner was telling the story in a more dramatic way: "I just heard that a boy fell into the canal and drowned!"

In less than half an hour, this terrible news spread from Beadzorr to Laklakon, where Asad and Samad lived, and then further to other communities. Everyone panicked because these areas had never experienced such a serious event. All of the parents rushed out to look for their children.

Asad's and Samad's mothers almost bumped into one another at the gate. They searched for their boys everywhere in Laklakon. They visited Burhon the Quince and Taheer-bobo, and even went to the Dushokh, but the boys were nowhere to be found.

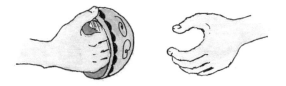

Meanwhile, an employee at the canal dam noticed a child's hat in the water and called the authorities. The green decorated hat was passed from one hand to the next. Everybody at the dam considered the hat as a piece of evidence worthy of further investigation. By that time, all of the parents had found all of their children—all except Asad and Samad. A search of the entire area was declared, and phones were ringing from house to house.

The farmers turned off their machines and gathered at the roads. Store owners were actively speaking to shoppers about the missing children.

Accountants and office clerks were looking at one another, but not working. Rescuers with all kinds of equipment rushed to the canal. The best swimmers volunteered to search the water. People abandoned the teahouses and cafeterias. The canal administrator suggested postponing the water supply to the canal for an hour.

The local radio station was broadcasting an emergency announcement:

"Two boys are lost. Their names are Asad and Samad." The radio also reported what they looked like, and even mentioned the dog Kalta.

Tavakkalhoja heard this news where he worked. "Where have those two mischief-makers gone?" he thought. "Ah, they will be back soon and their parents will teach them a lesson."

But then he grew doubtful. "What if, after I left, they returned to the canal? What if they really did fall in?"

Tavakkalhoja rushed to the community center to join the search for the boys. He was running so fast that very soon he passed the man on his bike. Embarrassed to be passed by a man on foot, the biker pedaled faster. It was funny to see a runner and a biker challenging one another.

Hasan was among those who observed this odd race. "Tavakkalhoja has lost his mind!" he declared. "No doubt about it!" So very soon another rumor followed the first one. In this rumor, Tavakkalhoja had lost his mind and was chasing anything on the road, even dogs, cats, and mice.

Asad and Samad in Good Spirits

Meanwhile, Asad and Samad were very happily walking along the canal. Why were they so happy? They were happy because soon they would find out where the water comes from. Indeed, where does the water come from?

The canal led them to a big building, from which came the noise of working machines. The boys could feel the ground shaking under their feet. This was the water pumping station. Three big pipes emerged from a wall of the building and turned toward the ground. From there a powerful rush of water was pouring into the canal.

"Here is where the water comes from!" Asad said.

The two friends were delighted about their discovery. Now they could go back home. One their way back, they encountered a group of children. They were in kindergarten, going on a field trip. Their teacher, a young and pretty lady, asked the students, "Who will tell me where the water comes from?"

Hearing this question, Asad and Samad stopped in their tracks.

The children began answering, one after the other:

"The water starts in the canal."

"The water comes from a stream."

"Our water is in a pool."

"The water comes from rain."

"No, from snow!"

"I know, I know! From ice!"

The teacher was waiting with a smile. Asad stepped closer and said, "Can I answer this question, please?"

"Certainly you can," the teacher said.

"The water comes from the station," Asad declared.

"And the rain and snow gather at the station," Samad added.

The other children were looking at Asad and Samad with admiration. The teacher said to them all, "It's true. The water in our canal comes from the water station, but it doesn't come directly from rain or snow, but from the river. You don't see the river because it is far from here, beyond the mountains. Its water comes here through the pipes. Then it goes out into the canal and from there to water ditches in all of the communities."

She wanted to tell more, but her voice was muffled by the noise of a motorbike. The motorbike hit its brakes, and Tavakkalhoja hopped off and came rushing toward the boys.

"Found at last!" he cried. "Found at last!"

Asad and Samad were given a seat in the sidecar, and Tavakkalhoja sat behind the driver. Kalta could just squeeze into the sidecar, too.

"Found at last! Found at last!" Tavakkalhoja kept repeating. As they rode home, they passed all the people they knew: Hasan the Fun, Burhon the Quince, and the mirab Muhammadjon.

Everyone was happy to see the boys safe, and they were greeting them all along the road. Asad and Samad thought that everybody was hailing them

because of their discovery. Asad and Samad, too, were shouting, "Found at last!" because they had found, at last, where the water comes from. Children were running after the motorbike, shouting the names of the two boys.

The phones stopped ringing. Farmers went back to work. Shop owners began to sell things again, and accountants returned to their calculations. Swimmers came out of the water. The local radio was playing music again. The mayor called the county government and told them that everything was under control.

Tavakkalhoja was proud that he had saved the girl and found the boys. Nobody can make fun of him anymore. Not even Hasan the Fun.

Everybody was happy. Well, our two friends got what they deserved from their parents. They were disciplined as needed. Nevertheless, Asad and Samad were happy, too, because at last they knew *where the water comes from!*

This story comes from Tajikistan, a small mountainous country that borders China, Afghanistan, Kyrgyzstan, and Uzbekistan in Central Asia. Formerly part of the Soviet Union, Tajikistan is now an independent nation. Most people there speak Tajik, a language related to Persian.

86

About the Author

Aminjon Khodjibaev, better known by his pen name Aminjon Shookuhi is one of the most prominent Tajik writers of the twentieth century. He was born in the Republic of Tajikistan in 1923 and grew up in the village of Rumon, a few miles away from the ancient city of Khujand. Khujand is referred to by historians as Alexandria Eskhata, where Alexander the Great founded a Hellenistic settlement, while leading his troops into Central Asia.

Aminjon Shookuhi made his debut as a young author in the late 1940's and was quickly recognized as a talented poet. His poems are considered some of the best in modern Tajik poetry. He later became a novelist and dramatist, and his work also includes a libretto for an opera, as well as classic Persian poetry forms.

Shookuhi wrote several collections of children's poetry and later published his trilogy, known primarily by the title of its first book "Where Does the Water Come From?" The story, set in Shookuhi's home village, represents a child's inherent sense of curiosity and desire to explore. The story also teaches everyone about the delicate nature of our environment.

Aminjon Shookuhi

Shookuhi was granted the highly coveted Rudaki Award and after his death was named the National Writer of Tajikistan. Facilities and streets bear his name in Tajikistan, and his statue is set in the front yard of the school where he once studied.

About the Translators

Karim Khodjibaev, the author's son, is a professional linguist who works in the field of adult education and language research. Together with his wife and co-authors, he published a large volume Tajik-English Dictionary. Some of his early publications are related to the socio-political dynamics of Central Asia. Khodjibaev holds an M.A. in linguistics and is a certified translator and interpreter in several languages.

Moukhabbat Khodjibaeva is the daughter-in-law of the author. She holds an M.A. in Cinema Arts and an M.S. in Information Technology. Moukhabbat works in the field of Eurasian studies and has written several articles dedicated to the history of women's life in that area. Moukhabbat specializes in curriculum development and has contributed to several language projects in both Persian and Russian.

Karim and Moukhabbat have a daughter and son and presently reside in the State of Virginia.

About the Illustrator

Jan Seabaugh is a teacher, poet, writer, and illustrator. She received her Ph.D. in Humanities from the University of Texas at Dallas and currently works in the writing program at St. Mary's College in South Bend, Indiana, where she lives with her husband, Alan.

Acknowledgements

We are extremely grateful to our lovely children, Azim and Sabrina, for their help and support in completing this project.

Our sincere thanks to Jan Seabaugh for her beautiful illustrations. Our special thanks to Viveca Smith.